# Unique Pets

# IGUANAS

Kristin Petrie

ABDO Publishing Company

## visit us at
## www.abdopublishing.com

Printed in the United States of America, North Mankato, Minnesota.
052012
092012

 PRINTED ON RECYCLED PAPER

Cover Photo: Photo Courtesy of Chris Shaw
Interior Photos: Corbis pp. 9, 21; Earl S. Cryer/UPI/Landov p. 19; Getty Images pp. 5, 7,
    10, 11, 14–15, 17; Pete Oxford/Minden Pictures/National Geographic Stock p. 13;
    Photo Researchers pp. 13, 17

Series Coordinator: Megan M. Gunderson
Editors: Megan M. Gunderson, BreAnn Rumsch
Art Direction: Neil Klinepier

### Library of Congress Cataloging-in-Publication Data

Petrie, Kristin, 1970-
  Iguanas / Kristin Petrie.
     p. cm. --  (Unique pets)
 Includes index.
  ISBN 978-1-61783-440-0
  1. Iguanas--Juvenile literature. 2. Iguanas as pets--Juvenile literature.  I. Title.
 QL666.L25P494 2013
 597.95'42--dc23

                      2012011504

---

### *Thinking about a Unique Pet?*
*Some communities have laws that regulate the ownership of unique pets. Be sure
to check with your local authorities before buying one of these special animals.*

# CONTENTS

# IGUANAS

What animals look like small dragons, live in the treetops, and love to swim? Some of these unusual creatures will walk on a leash. Happy ones can stick around for more than 20 years. Give up? They're iguanas!

Iguanas are from the scientific family Iguanidae, which includes about 700 species. One species in particular has become a common pet. This is *Iguana iguana,* or the green iguana.

Chances are you have seen a green iguana or maybe even held one. You may have a friend that has this pet. Or perhaps you care for your own!

The green iguana became a popular pet in the 1990s. At that time, iguanas were captured in the

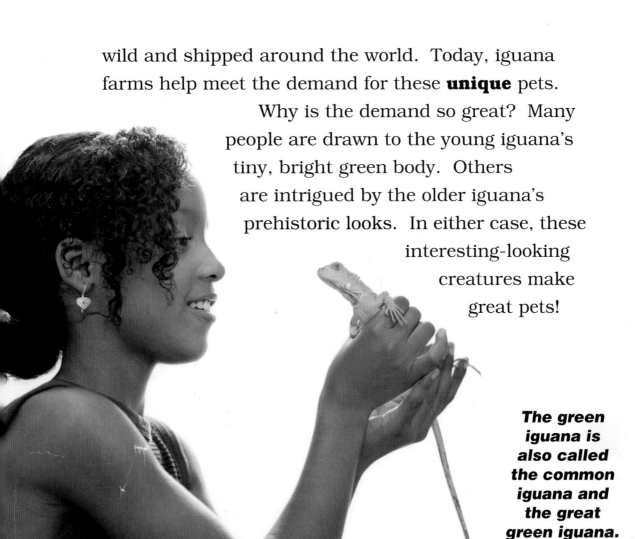

wild and shipped around the world. Today, iguana farms help meet the demand for these **unique** pets.

Why is the demand so great? Many people are drawn to the young iguana's tiny, bright green body. Others are intrigued by the older iguana's prehistoric looks. In either case, these interesting-looking creatures make great pets!

*The green iguana is also called the common iguana and the great green iguana.*

# WHERE THEY LIVE

Iguanas are native to Mexico, Central America, and South America. They also live on Caribbean islands and have been introduced in Hawaii and Florida. Today, more iguanas live outside of their native regions than in them!

What do all of these places have in common? Heat! The iguana is an ectothermic animal. So, it needs heat from its **environment** to maintain its body temperature. The areas bordering rain forests provide the perfect temperature for the iguana to successfully grow and reproduce.

Iguanas are also **arboreal**. They live in the rain forest **canopy**. The iguana's simple home is a branch in the sun! This high-rise **habitat** gives the iguana easy access to the sun's warm rays. It also provides plentiful shade when the iguana needs to cool down.

With such a perfect home, the iguana rarely comes to the ground.

# DEFENSE

The iguana's lofty lodging provides pluses other than warmth. Its **arboreal** home is safe from ground-dwelling predators. Still, some tree-loving creatures prey on the iguana. These include snakes, birds, and other lizards.

When predators come around, the iguana's best defense is to freeze! The motionless iguana's **camouflaged** skin helps it blend in with the surrounding greenery.

If its predator can see through this disguise, the iguana can try to be scary. It will use its tail as a whip or deliver a painful bite. If all else fails, the iguana will escape by jumping off its branch. Just in case, these smart lizards often **bask** on branches that hang over water!

Unfortunately, there are some threats iguanas cannot escape. Some people hunt iguanas for their meat and skin. Iguanas also suffer from **habitat** destruction. Efforts to reduce deforestation help protect iguanas from extinction.

### THE PET TRADE

*In some areas, iguanas are taken from their natural habitats to be sold as pets. To protect wild populations of iguanas, many pets now come from farms. These captive-bred pets adapt more easily to life with humans. They're less likely to react aggressively to being handled. This is good for owners too, because iguanas can bite!*

# WHAT THEY LOOK LIKE

Scales, spines, and bumps, oh my! Iguanas have some interesting physical features. Baby iguanas attract attention with their bright green coloring. They are tiny and cute, but not for long! Adults can grow 6.6 feet (2 m) long and weigh 13.2 pounds (6 kg)! Males are larger than females.

*A cold iguana's skin will darken to better absorb the sun's rays. An overheated iguana's skin will lighten in color to deflect rays.*

This substantial lizard's body features a broad head and a short snout. Two small eyes set far apart offer a wide field of vision. A soft flap of skin called the dewlap hangs from the iguana's throat.

Long legs and clawed feet make this lizard a fast runner and an impressive climber. The long, tapered tail does double duty. It provides balance in the trees and acts as a propeller in the water.

An adult iguana's color varies widely from green to orange. It even changes due to temperature, mood, and health.

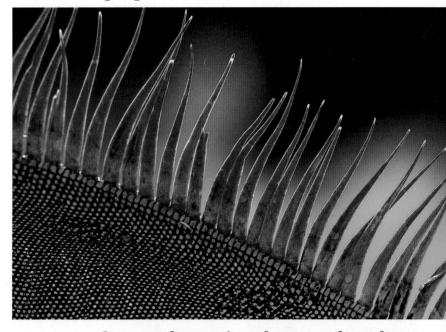

**A green iguana's spines run from its neck to the base of its tail.**

# BEHAVIORS

Lazy might be the best description for an iguana. Its number one activity is **basking** in the sun. This doesn't just help it stay warm. Staying still also conserves its energy. The iguana's diet is healthy, but low in calories. So, it moves slowly and rests a lot!

Still, an iguana can get a move on when it needs to. It will battle to save a favorite perch. A male will also behave **aggressively** if its territory or mate is approached. An angry iguana bobs its head, bites, extends its dewlap, and changes color.

What if an enemy has a hold on its tail? Then the iguana uses its secret weapon. It can detach its tail! This distracts its clueless enemy and allows the iguana to flee.

An iguana's senses also help it detect and dodge danger. It relies heavily on its vision and sense of smell. Iguanas also have excellent hearing.

**The iguana also counts on its parietal eye. This spot on its head helps it detect light and dark, such as the shadow of a predator passing by.**

*A new, shorter tail will grow in about a year's time to replace a lost one.*

# FOOD

You already know iguanas love sunbathing. Their second favorite activity is eating! In fact, iguanas spend most of their day in a pattern of eating, resting, and **digesting**.

Iguanas are mainly herbivores. Leaves, blossoms, and fruits from trees and shrubs are their favorite snacks. Young iguanas need more **protein** than adults due to their rapid growth. So they enjoy insects and spiders, too!

A pet iguana needs to eat a diet similar to that of its wild relatives. The diet should include

dark leafy greens, fruits, and grains. Variety is key. Your iguana should have at least ten different items throughout the course of the week!

These foods should be chopped up and offered to your iguana each morning. This allows your pet to follow its natural pattern of daytime munching and resting. And don't forget, fresh water should always be available.

**_Resting allows iguanas to direct their energy toward digesting their leafy foods._**

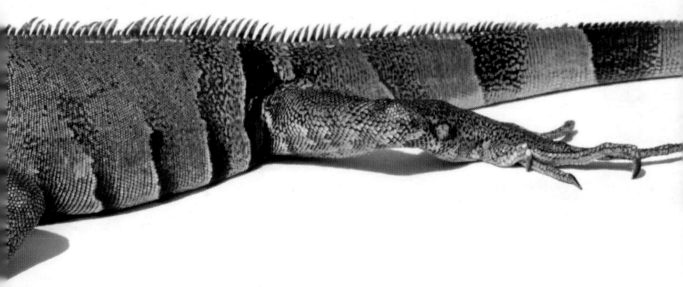

# REPRODUCTION

Just how do these bright green creatures enter the world?  It all starts when iguanas reach maturity, which happens between three and four years of age.

A male attracts a female by showing off his dashing dewlap and bobbing head!  After mating, fertilized eggs develop inside the female's body for about 65 days.

After this time, the female does something unusual.  She makes her way down to the forest floor!  There, she creates a burrow and deposits up to 65 eggs into it.  This hard work can take as many as three days.  But after the last egg is laid, her work is done.  She returns to her home high in the **canopy**.

*Young iguanas are independent at birth and quickly find a home in the trees.  But they stay on lower branches, because adults claim the highest perches!*

Meanwhile, the eggs develop in their cozy burrow. After another 90 to 120 days, fully developed baby iguanas emerge from their shells.

It is best to wait to adopt a pet iguana until it is three to five months old. At this age, an iguana is strong and healthy. But it's not too old for training!

# CARE

Before adopting a cute little iguana, certain questions must be answered. First, can you have an iguana where you live? Some cities do not allow them as pets. Second, is there a reptile veterinarian nearby? It can be hard to find someone with experience treating iguanas.

Finally, do you have what it takes to own an iguana? It's a big responsibility! An iguana's daily supply of fresh fruits and vegetables can be expensive. It also needs fresh water daily and frequent misting in order to stay **hydrated**. And it can carry salmonella bacteria, which can make people sick.

You'll also have to groom your iguana. Its toenails will need trimming. And occasionally, it will need help **shedding** its outgrown skin. These good swimmers also enjoy a daily bath!

Iguanas need love, attention, and patience. When young, many iguanas do not like to be held. However, daily handling will help your new pet become used to you. Some iguanas will never become tame. But others can learn to walk on a leash or sit on your shoulder!

*Training your iguana requires patience.*

# THINGS THEY NEED

Have you decided you can't live without an iguana? That's great! Now you'll need to prepare a home for your new arrival.

A young iguana will feel at home in a glass aquarium. However, a fully grown iguana needs a large cage. The cage must have enough space for moving and climbing. And, it must be tall enough to contain branches and plants.

Since iguanas are ectothermic, they need a place for **basking**. Heat and access to **UV** light can come from the sun or from special lamps. Equally important is a place to cool off. Plants and branches create shade and cooler areas.

Temperatures in the cage should range from 75 to 95 degrees Fahrenheit (24 to 35°C).

Caring for an iguana may seem like a lot of work. But it can be worth it! A healthy, happy iguana can be an enjoyable companion for more than 20 years.

**Your iguana's home will need weekly cleaning.**

# GLOSSARY

**aggressive** (uh-GREH-sihv) - displaying hostility.

**arboreal** (ahr-BAWR-ee-uhl) - living in or frequenting trees.

**bask** - to lie in a pleasant warmth, such as the sun.

**camouflage** - relating to hiding or disguising something by covering it up or changing its appearance.

**canopy** - the uppermost spreading, branchy layer of a forest.

**digest** - to break down food into simpler substances the body can absorb.

**environment** - all the surroundings that affect the growth and well-being of a living thing.

**habitat** - a place where a living thing is naturally found.

**hydrated** - supplied with ample fluid or water.

**protein** - a substance which provides energy to the body and serves as a major class of foods for animals. Foods high in protein include cheese, eggs, fish, meat, and milk.

**shed** - to cast of hair, feathers, skin, or other coverings
or parts by a natural process.

**unique** - being the only one of its kind.

**UV** - ultraviolet. These rays of light cannot be seen.
They can come from the sun or from special lamps.

# WEB SITES

To learn more about iguanas, visit ABDO Publishing
Company online. Web sites about iguanas are featured
on our Book Links page. These links are routinely
monitored and updated to provide the most current
information available.

**www.abdopublishing.com**

# INDEX